GOD'S MASTERPIECE

A PORTRAIT OF THE BORN-AGAIN SPIRIT

HERBERT ERIC FEARMAN

Published by Revival House Books
14572 Walking stick way
Strongsville Ohio 44136

Ministry Information
Herbert Eric Fearman
efearman@yahoo.com
440-494-1859
Revival House Network You tube

Interior Book Design / Layout
CBM Christian Book Editing
www.christian-book-editing.com

Table of Contents

Introduction

This work focuses on a very important subject that's not taught or studied very often despite being significant enough to be shouted from mountain tops. Remember what Jesus told us in John 3:3 and John 3:5: Except a man be born again he can not see the kingdom of God and Except a man be born of water and of the Holy Spirit he can not enter the kingdom of God. We should all know more about this glorious new creation that has taken place within every spirit-filled believer of Jesus Christ. I'm sure that even with my extensive research and the countless hours of study invested on this subject, I've only just begun to scratch the surface of this topic. After you read and mediate on the findings of this book, I believe the New Testament will become clearer and more rewarding to you. Discovering the things that God has already bestowed on us is truly amazing, and it's even more mind-blowing to realize what he deposited within us when we submitted our lives to his son Jesus. God almighty has a glorious fellowship with us right now in heavenly places that we know nothing about, but he's just beginning to pull back the curtain and offer us glimpses. The things he has done just to make sure our communion with him will never again be broken is truly remarkable. This book is a short and easy read filled with revelation knowledge and power. By the design of the Holy Spirit, this book lets the Bible do the talking instead of providing opinions. I love it when the scriptures breath fresh revelation, and the revelation in this book paints a lovely portrait of the born-again spirit.

Chapter 1

Getting to Know Yourself

1 Thessalonians 5:23

And the very God of peace sanctify you wholly; and I pray God your whole spirit and soul and body be preserved blameless unto the coming of our Lord Jesus Christ.

In this wonderful prayer, Paul describes the total makeup of mankind—spirit, soul and body. We are first a spirit, we have a soul, and we reside in a physical body.

spirit = life in the spiritual realm

soul = mind will emotion

body = physical life

When Adam and Eve ate from the tree of the knowledge of good and evil, though they didn't die physically till hundreds of years later, they did experience an immediate spiritual death. Death doesn't translate to non-existence; it means separation. They were spiritually separated from God when they descended into sin, and the price of sin is death. With **physical death,** the spirit and soul leave the body, going to hell or to the presence of Jesus as the body returns to dust. **Spiritual death** occurs at birth, and the spirit, soul and body are disconnected from their Creator. They continue to live dominated by evil. This is the state we are all born into. There's a difference in spiritual and physical death, with spiritual death being far worse because there is no life after being disconnected from God—only an existence dominated by Satan.

Psalms 51:5 NLT

For I was born a sinner- yes, from the moment my mother conceived me.

We were born into this sinful condition because spiritual death was passed down to us by Adam, but the good news is that there is one who has walked this earth without Adam's DNA.

1 Corinthians 15:22 NLT

Just as everyone dies because we all belong to Adam, everyone who belongs to Jesus Christ will be given NEW LIFE.

Jesus' father was not Adam—it was God, and he was sinless. God's DNA enabled him to walk this earth in the flesh without sin and therefore, he condemned sin in the flesh so that the righteousness of the law might be fulfilled in us who trust in Jesus Christ as our Lord and savior. Doing that helps us escape spiritual death and returns us in fellowship with our heavenly Father Jehovah.

Romans 8:2

For the law of the Spirit of life in Christ Jesus hath made me free from the law of sin and death.

When we turn to Jesus with all our hearts, our darkened and frail human spirit becomes full of eternal life and power. This is what Jesus called being born again.

John 3:3

Except a man be born again he can not enter the kingdom of God.

Studying and experiencing this spiritual rebirth has been immensely rewarding for me and my ministry, and the truths that I'm going to share in this book will radically change your life if you meditate on them.

2 Corinthians 5:17

Therefore if any man be in Christ, he is a new creature: old things are passed away; behold, all things are become new.

Notice how Paul says **"old things are passed away"**— an expression made in the past tense, coupled with **"all things are become new"** a statement made in the present tense. This verse confused me for some time; I knew I had been born again, but I still struggled with bad thoughts from time to time. I still suffered from a bad temper, and I struggled with my flesh. The same old sicknesses attacked my body, and the same old devil tried to influence my mind. Then one day, the Lord gave me the revelation—Paul was referring to my new spirit man. I then realized that this new creation occurred in the spiritual part of my being, outside of my five senses and in another dimension. Negative thoughts and feelings are of the soul where the mind and emotions reside and do not belong to the spirit. And one day, the Holy Ghost led me to this verse:

1 Corinthians 6:17

But he that is joined unto the Lord is one spirit.

This verse told me that upon conversion, my weak human spirit merged with the omnipotent, omnipresent, omniscient Holy Spirit by my submission to Christ and now I understand that "I can do all things through Christ that strengthens me." My reborn spirit can receive directly from God's omnipotence, and all things become possible for me. Being one with the Holy Spirit lends me capabilities that extend beyond what I can ask for or think of and according to the power that's working in me (**my spirit man.**)

1 Peter 1:23

Being born again, not of corruptible seed, but of incorruptible, by the word of God, which lives and abides for ever.

The Greek term for seed is "spora"; it's literally translated to **parentage or origin.**

The origin of my new spirit man is in God. I carry God's DNA in my spirit and therefore, my spirit is like God or of a God-kind, who is incorruptible, eternal, almighty and perfect in all of his ways. The rebirth occurred because God spoke it so—"<u>by the word or logos of God.</u>" God said Let there be a new class of mankind that will act and think and experience me so closely that they will think like I think, know what I know, talk like I talk, and feel what I feel. GLORY!!! But please remember that this is the you in your spirit who occupies another dimension. Later in this book, we will learn how to accord preeminence to our spirit and **allow him to have dominance in our lives.** Recall what Jesus taught us in John 3:6—"That which is born of flesh is flesh and that which is born of spirit is spirit." We have an **earthly birth** and a **heavenly birth,** and it's through God's Word that we see into the heavenly realm. Let's consider Titus 3:5 and continue studying this marvelous spiritual baptism.

Not by works of righteousness which we have done, but according to his mercy he saved us, by the washing of regeneration, and renewing of the Holy Ghost.

God saved us with the **washing** or **baptism** of **regeneration** or **rebirth**, and the **renewing of the Holy Ghost**. Let's try to simplify this.

"Baptism of rebirth and renewing of the Holy Ghost." This section breaks down the process of rebirth further. Our weak and darkened human spirit is baptized into Christ or anointed and we never get out of the pool! As a matter of fact, we even drink it. As kids, we were taught never to drink pool water but this isn't just any water—this is the living water of life that Jesus talked about.

John 7:37

In the last day, that great day of the feast, Jesus stood and cried, saying, **If any man thirst, let him come unto me, and drink.**

John 7:38

He that believes on me, as the scripture hath said, out of his belly shall **flow rivers of living water.**

1 Corinthians 12:13

For by one Spirit are we all baptized into one body, whether we be Jews or Gentiles, whether we be bond or free; **and have been all made to drink into one Spirit.**

My spirit is in Christ, and Christ is in my spirit. I am united with the believers in one Body. I am one spirit with the Holy Spirit, and I am born in the origin of God with His DNA in me. I am baptized and made to drink in God's Holy Spirit. I am more than a Conqueror through him who loves me. Spiritual baptism immersed me in the river of life and now I am in Christ, and my spirit man drinks of the river and Christ is in me and out of my spirit flow the rivers of living water.

Galatians 3:27

*For as many of you as have been baptized into Christ **have put on Christ.***

The reborn spirit wears Christ or the anointing as a garment, and I believe this garment of Christ on the spirit man shines with a light so bright that demons have to retreat and bow and worship. It's not us that they bow down to but the garment of God that we wear in the spirit.

Romans 13:12

*The night is far spent, the day is at hand: let us therefore cast off the works of darkness, **and let us put on the armour of light.***

Ephesians 5:8

*For ye were sometimes darkness, **but now are ye light in the Lord: walk as children of light:***

Ephesians 5:14

*Wherefore he saith, Awake thou that sleepest, and arise from the dead, **and Christ shall give thee light.***

1 Thessalonians 5:5

***Ye are all the children of light,** and the children of the day: we are not of the night, nor of darkness.*

Romans 8:15

For ye have not received the spirit of bondage again to fear; but ye have received the Spirit of adoption, whereby we cry, Abba, Father.

When we were physically born into this world, we spiritually died to God and we were led by our five senses and bound in sin and fear. Recall the episode where God called Adam after he ate the forbidden fruit. Adam hid from God for the very first time and even said that he was afraid of Him. Fear belongs to the realm of darkness where everyone is afraid—even the devil. At birth and beyond are the spirits who are fearful of death, fearful of evil and fearful of God because of sin. But now, being born again, I possess the spirit of sonship and in my spirit, I know now that I belong to God. I can call him **Abba,** which means **daddy**. Abba is one of the first words I heard in Church in the midst of worship as the spirits of the saints cried out to God with love and passion.

Romans 8:16

The Spirit itself bears witness with our spirit, that we are the children of God.

The mere fact that God's Spirit has merged with our spirit testifies that we are God's children forever and that we will always be with the Lord.

Ephesians 2:10 NLT

*We are **God's masterpiece**. He has created us anew in Christ Jesus, so we can do the good things he planned for us long ago.*

Chapter 2

Sinless and Perfect

1 John 3:9

Whosoever is born of God doth not commit sin; for his seed remains in him: and he cannot sin, because he is born of God.

Here we have the Apostle John telling us that the born-again spirit in us is sinless and perfected in Christ. This is so wonderful because God reserved a place in us where he can form a fellowship and commune with His children. Just as it is impossible for God to sin, it is impossible for us to sin with our spirits because **God's seed is in us.**

Remember what Peter taught us?

1 Peter 1:23

(Being born again, not of corruptible seed, but of incorruptible, by the word of God, which lives and abides for ever.)

John takes it a step further and adopts another related Greek term for seed, *sperma*—**the root word of the English term "sperm."**

1 John 3:9

*Whosoever is born of God doth not commit sin; for his **seed** remains in him: and he cannot sin, because he is born of God.*

John tells us that God's **sperma remains in us. So, it is impossible for our spirit man to ever commit any sin .**

God put his **reproductive cells** in our spirit to ensure reproduction after **his kind,** implying that our reborn spirit is developing in God's character and likeness. As we continue to dwell on these powerful truths about our spirit man, our minds will begin yielding to the work of grace done in our spirits and our spirits will occupy their rightful place as our leader and commander on the earth.

2 Corinthians 4:7

But we have this treasure in earthen vessels, that the excellency of the power may be of God, and not of us.

Our new spirit man's power to live sinless emerges from God's seed that He planted within us at rebirth. It gives us complete access to the throne of God. Because God is a Spirit, and we must worship him with our spirit and follow the truth of his word. The only worship from us that's acceptable to God is the one made through the spirit he birthed in us the day we completely placed our trust in Jesus as our Lord and Savior. The excellency of power that's in our spirit man is God's power and not ours. Our spirit will only release this power in the earth according to God's will and his will alone (It's not from us, it's from him).

Ephesians 4:24

And that ye put on the new man, which after God is created in righteousness and true holiness.

Paul, by the revelation of the Holy Ghost, is telling us that this new creation is **after God;** in other words, it's **from God and** it's **like God**. What I intend to claim here is that the New Testament is full of revelations about this wonderful thing that God has done in us! Created after God in righteousness and true holiness! Within us is righteousness, holiness, power, truth, glory and much more, and I pray for the day the Church starts proclaiming these truths and disseminates them all across this world.

2 Corinthians 5:21

For he hath made him to be sin for us, who knew no sin; that we might be made the righteousness of God in him.

Let's focus on the phrase **"might be made"** in the quote above. The phrasing in Greek uses the term "ginomai" that means to **generate** or **reproduce** or **procreate.**

Our spirit is not created to do righteousness; it is created to **be righteous.** It is created for the Kingdom of God, which is the abode of righteousness, peace and joy in the Holy Ghost.

1John 4:17

Herein is our love made perfect, that we may have boldness in the day of judgment: because as he is, so are we in this world.

This, child of God, this is wonderful assurance knowing that at the present time on planet earth we are like Him in his holiness, wisdom, power and so on! Knowing that assures me that I will be with him forever, and it gives me courage in my trials and tribulations in this life and will ensure my victory in the next one. We are like him because he loves us and he doesn't want sin or guilt to break our fellowship ever again.

Romans 7:22

For I delight in the law of God after the inward man

Our reborn spirit has no problem obeying God's law any more than Jesus did when he walked this earth, but what we must understand is that when we do sin, it's not committed by our spirit man but **by the flesh** and that **old sinful nature** should be **crucified daily**.

Romans 7:23

But I see another law in my members, warring against the law of my mind, and bringing me into captivity to the law of sin which is in my members.

In this passage, Paul is referring to the physical body being controlled by the **carnal or flesh-dictated mind** with the term "**members**." All of humanity is born under the law of sin and death and that includes our spirit, soul, and body. This is why we must be b**orn again of the Spirit** and our minds must be renewed and our bodies must be glorified to inhabit the new earth and the new heaven.

Galatians 5:22+23

But the fruit of the Spirit is love, joy, peace, patience, gentleness, goodness, faith, Meekness, temperance: against such there is no law.

Galatians 5:25

If we live in the Spirit, let us also walk in the Spirit.

Being born again is the life of our spirit man which is filled with the **fruit of the Holy Spirit.** Paul is merely advising us that since this is our new life, let's experience it in our entire beings. We have to allow it to come forward by crucifying our flesh **(the old man)**. As we learn to avoid sin and evil, the flesh will starve and weaken and the spirit will naturally emerge and situate itself at the center of your life. The fruit of the Holy Spirit is the new nature of our reborn spirit.

*We are **God's masterpiece**. He has created us anew in Christ Jesus, so we can do the good things he planned for us long ago.*

Chapter 3
Daily Updates

1Corithians 2:6

For who hath known the mind of the Lord, that he may instruct him? **But we have the mind of Christ.**

Within our new created spirit resides a new mind; Paul labels it the mind of Christ. Our human spirit is baptized into the spirit of Christ, and he drinks Christ and now we're able to think like Christ. Notice that Paul says that we don't instruct the Lord, thereby implying that we will never be as intelligent as God **but we do hold his mind** in our recreated spirit. Once our old mind starts submitting to these truths, it will also resign itself to the mind of Christ, which is the mind of our born-again spirit man. It will merge in submission just as how our old spirit did to our born-again spirit. When our new spirit man bearing the mind of Christ joins the glorified body at the Rapture of the Church, God will be all in all concerning his Church.

Ezekiel 36:26

A new heart also will I give you, and a new spirit will I put within you:

Ezekiel 36:27

And I will put my spirit within you, and cause you to walk in my statutes, and ye shall keep my judgments, and do them.

Proverb 27:3 states "**as a man thinks in is heart so is he.**" The new heart being spoken of here is a new mind and then a new spirit. This ancient prophecy speaks of the new creation that's available to every person on this planet today and which is designed to lead us to walk in God's statutes and keep his judgments. With God, obedience is better than any sacrifice we could ever offer him; therefore, he assisted us by gifting us his divine nature.

2 Peter 1:4

Whereby are given unto us exceeding great and precious promises: that by these ye might be partakers of the divine nature, having escaped the corruption that is in the world through lust.

The exceeding great and precious promises mentioned above are what we have been studying in this book so far; they are designed to make our minds aware of these truths, thereby allowing us to be partakers or to experience the divine nature of God in us. Our minds are only renewed by submitting to truth. We will dive deeper into this in a later chapter. Now that we have comprehensively established that the mind of Christ is the mind of our born-again spirit man, let's pursue this matter further and delve into it more extensively.

2 Corinthians 4:16

*For which cause we faint not; but though our outward man perish, yet the **inward man** is **renewed** day by day.*

Paul is definitely raising a credible argument here; yes, we are getting older in our physical forms, but we have an inward man who has the mind of Christ which gets renewed day after day.

The Greek term for renewed is **"anakainoo"**; it means to **renovate.** To renovate something implies **making improvements** or **making updates** to it. The Bible is telling us that these updates occur every day, which means that **we**

are progressing in divine knowledge daily in our born-again spirits.

Col 3:10

*And have put on the **new man,** which is **renewed in knowledge** after the image of him that created him:*

Our recreated spirit is updated daily with divine knowledge, and this divine knowledge is molding and making us more and more like our heavenly Father. This is an eternal process, implying that throughout all eternity, we will keep growing and advancing in Godlike character and intellect. There will never ever be a fall again because it's impossible for this new form created in Christ Jesus to sin similar to how it's impossible for God to sin. We were born again only to do good deeds. Remember, old things have passed away and all things have become new. This means that the old pattern or formation in the beginning of our creation is rejected and a new formation has occupied its space as we now walk the path of a new life, being born again not of corruptible seed but the incorruptible and divine nature of God Almighty. The Greek term for **knowledge** in this context also means **supreme intelligence** and it's being given to our spirit man daily so that we would know the things that are freely given to us by our heavenly Father.

1 Corinthians 2:12

Now we have received, not the spirit of the world, **but the spirit which is of God;** *that we might know the things that are freely given to us of God.*

Our spirit man holds information about the several wonderful things that we possess and of which we are not aware; hence, it's important that we learn these truths about rebirth and meditate on them daily. There is no faith without the knowledge of truth; you must first know to believe and once you know and believe God's truth, you can experience all the spiritual blessings in Christ.

Ephesians 1:2

Blessed be the God and Father of our Lord Jesus Christ, who hath blessed us with all spiritual blessings in heavenly places in Christ:

Our born-again spirit man is baptized in Christ, drinks Christ, abides in Christ and receives all spiritual blessings. Emphasis should be placed here on the phrase **"All Spiritual**

Blessings." There aren't any spiritual blessings that God has not spoken over our spirits.

1 Corinthians 2:9+10

But as it is written, Eye hath not seen, nor ear heard, neither have entered into the heart of man, the things which God hath prepared for them that love him.

But God hath revealed them unto us by his Spirit: for the Spirit searches all things, yea, the deep things of God.

We cannot see these things, we cannot hear these things, we cannot even think these things with our minds unless they are given to us by way of our spirit man.

Our new spirit wants so badly to reveal these things to us, **but we must start by understanding who he is;** that's what we've been doing so far and will continue doing.

1 Corinthians 2:15

The one who is spiritual discerns all things, yet he himself is understood by no one.

As we've learned, **our born-again spirit man is replenished daily with supreme intelligence,** and this intelligence covers all of space and time and every dimension. Our spirit, equipped with this supreme knowledge, can discern everything because it's after the very image of God. Meaning is thus birthed with his omniscience. Our spirit knows about things in heaven as well as the things on earth, and this is very useful to us as we navigate through this life. But notice that no one can discern our spirit, not even us. While our spirit knows everything about our soul and body, the only way we can know about him is through **God's word and the Holy Spirit**. God's word is a lovely window that offers a view of the spirit man. However, it's all in reverse. This implies that **knowledge comes before the view;** in other words, **we know and then we see and experience** whereas in the physical world, **we see and then we analyze what we see and decide**. We gain knowledge about our spirit to experience eternal life today.

Hebrews 4:12

> *For the word of God is quick, and powerful, and sharper than any two edged sword, piercing even to the dividing asunder of soul and spirit, and of the joints and marrow, and is a judge of the thoughts and intents of the heart.*

It is only though God's Word that we can begin to discern our spirit man; the Word sits between the soul and the spirit as a picture window until that which is perfect arrives and then we will know even as we are known, 1 Corinthians 13:12. It's through God's Word that we learn about who we really are in this wonderful, new creation.

This is what seek to undertake in this book. We look not at the **things that are seen** but at the **things that are not seen** for the things which are seen are **temporal** but the things which are not seen are **eternal.**

Chapter 4

No Boundaries

John 3:8 NIV

The wind blows wherever it pleases. You hear its sound, but you cannot tell where it comes from or where it is going. **So it is with everyone born of the Spirit.**

In the quote provided above, Jesus is making a comparison between our newly created spirit and the wind. He is informing us that born-again spirits can travel wherever they please just like God, from heaven to hell, from planet earth to the edge of this universe, and through seen or unseen realms. Take note here of the phrase "we cannot tell where it comes from or where it is going." As we start to truly walk in the spirit, we must rely on faith and divine revelation. This brings to mind the old saying "my momma didn't raise no fool!" After meditating on these scriptural truths about power and glory of our born-again spirit man, our minds will soon desire to submit to the mind of Christ and the leadership of our spirit man through faith, confession and sanctification;

when that happens, the unity of self will be established, followed by the gaining of power and virtue.

Ephesians 3:20

Now unto him that is able to do exceeding abundantly above all that we ask or think, according to the power that works in us,

God operates far beyond our mental capacity and in things that we've never thought of nor spoken about. He brings these wonderful blessings to us by way of his miraculous power that dwells in our spirit man. He works from within us and not outside of us because he has already created a meeting place within our born-again spirit which has become an extension of himself. Remember, **"He that is joined to the Lord is one spirit"**

Ephesians 2:5+6

Even when we were dead in sins, hath quickened us together with Christ, (by grace ye are saved;)

*And hath raised us up together, **and made us sit together in heavenly places in Christ Jesus:***

We may be physically present on planet earth and our spirit may be in heaven before the throne of God because our born-again spirit has access to **God's omnipresence**. A part of us is extremely familiar with heaven and earth. I can't explain this phenomenon, but I have faith in it. Why? Because the Bible says it's so. But one thing I do know is that my spirit experiences this by the grace of God.

John 3:13

And no man hath ascended up to heaven, but he that came down from heaven, even the Son of man which is in heaven.

Now I know this blew Nicodemus' mind because it blows my mind centuries later. Let me translate this for you! Jesus is saying that **"no man has independently ascended up to heaven but me the one that came down from heaven, the Son of man who is also in heaven right now!"** **God's omnipresence** is available to our spirit man!

Hebrews 12:22-24

But ye are *come unto mount Sion, and unto the city of the living God, the heavenly Jerusalem, and to an innumerable company of angels, To the general assembly and church of the firstborn, which are written in heaven,* *and to God the Judge of all, **and to the spirits of just men made perfect,** And to Jesus the mediator of the new covenant, and to the blood of sprinkling, that speaketh better things than that of Abel.*

Just as sure as we've come to the blood of Jesus and the new covenant, we have also come to Mount Zion, the heavenly Jerusalem through our spirit man. Remember what Jesus told—**our born-again spirit man goes where he pleases.** We are citizens now! Not when he comes for us! Our citizenship is established now because our spirits visit heaven frequently. Notice (and to the spirits of just men made perfect), **this includes the us today** as well as those who physically sleep in Jesus. The Holy Spirit is not telling us that we've come to resurrected men with glorified bodies; he is saying that we've come to the perfected spirits of men and that's a sign that this scripture is for today before the rapture.

Philippians 3:20+21 NLT

But we are citizens of heaven, where the Lord Jesus Christ lives. And we are eagerly waiting for him to return as our Savior.

Who shall change our vile body, that it may be fashioned like unto his glorious body, according to the

One day soon, we will receive our glorified bodies to house our born-again spirits; then, we will be ready for eternity. PRAISE GOD!

Chapter 5

The Spirit's Language

Spiritual birth is, in some manner, similar to natural birth. When the newborn comes out of the womb, the doctors need to hear the baby's cry.

So is it when one is born again; there is a sound in a heavenly language that comes forth. This is not a fixed phenomenon but does occur predominantly. I do know some who are born again and have never spoken in this heavenly language; but their lives bear the fruit of the Spirit. I tell them all the time that they don't know what they are missing!

1 Corinthians 14:14

For if I pray in an unknown tongue, my spirit prayeth, but my understanding is unfruitful.

This is very important to see and understand. Paul says **"my spirit prayeth."** Child of God, this communication between God and our born-again spirit is vital since it assists us in walking in the gifts of the Spirit, walking in the wisdom of God, and walking in the power of God. Notice Paul's words—**"my understanding is unfruitful."** This language is strictly used between God and His children. Other creatures in the spirit realm such as demons don't understand it either—it's a private exchange! We speak out so many of our thoughts daily—some are beneficial and some aren't. But words spoken from within after rebirth benefit us in all ways possible. Good things happen when we allow our spirits to speak on the earth. Remember our words set the course of our lives, and death and life are in the power of the tongue.

1 Corinthians 14:4

He that speaketh in an unknown tongue edifieth himself; but he that prophesieth edifieth the church.

When our spirits pray to God in this heavenly language, it edifies us. The Greek term for edifieth also means **"build or embolden."** Speaking in an unknown tongue strengthens our born-again spirit and gives it the courage to face any challenge. It's similar to bulking up on spiritual muscles!

Jude 1:20

*But ye, beloved, **building up yourselves** on your most holy faith, **praying in the Holy Ghost,***

1 John 5:18

*We know that whosoever is born of God sinneth not; but he that is begotten of God **keepeth himself,** and that wicked one toucheth him not.*

Our sinless born-again spirit is so empowered by God that Satan himself cannot touch him. It says **he keepeth himself.** In Greek, the term "keepeth" means to **guard and protect**. Prior to its new creation, our spirits were darkened and disconnected from the life of God and Satan had power over us and that power was sin and death.

But now, the Spirit of life in Jesus Christ has freed me from the laws of sin and death, and the righteousness of the law is fulfilled in us who are born of the Spirit of God.

The devil cannot touch our spirit anymore; they are free to go to hell if they want to and not be touched by any evil   spirit!

1 Cor 14:2

*For he that speaketh in an unknown tongue speaketh not unto men, but unto God: for no man understandeth him; howbeit **in the spirit he speaketh mysteries**.*

This heavenly conversation between God and our spirit man is a mystery to our minds but not to our spirits; through diligent prayers, however, we can receive revelation in our mind. When I pray in tongue, there have been times when I have received wisdom from God as well as answers to questions in my mind that I had not prayed about before. Another wonderful thing about our heavenly language is that it portrays the trinity. I can speak in tongues with my **spirit** while reading a book with my **mind** and walking through the house with my **body**. The Lord has also blessed me with English terms that emerge from within my spirit in prayer. This is another level of love and compassion for Jesus. There have been times during prayer when my spirit took over in English and spoke praises to the Godhead with such love and compassion that I felt the intensity of those words surge all through my body. It's as if all of my born-again spirit only thinks about Jesus; all he desires is Jesus; all he cares about is

Jesus. This is a level of passion that extends beyond the limits of this world!

James 4:5 NLT

Or do you think Scripture says without reason that **he jealously longs for the spirit he has caused to dwell in us**

I understand this verse better now because of the supernatural love that not only flows out of our spirits to God but also flows back into our spirit man from our heavenly Father.

It's truly amazing how God brought us to this place of purity and righteousness so that we can share unbroken communion with Him throughout all eternity.

1 Corinthians 14:18

I thank my God, I speak with tongues more than ye all:

I believe that praying in unknown tongues was one of the Apostle Paul's greatest secrets to success. Here, he boasts that he speaks in more tongues than the entire church in Corinth. Building and empowering your spirit man by this heavenly communication is truly wonderful; blessings are words that come from the mouth of God directly to our spirits and God always prospers his word.

Isaiah 28:11+12

*For with stammering lips and another tongue **will he speak to this people.***

*To whom he said, **This is the rest** wherewith ye may cause the **weary to rest;** and this is **the refreshing**: yet they would not hear.*

Notice verse eleven tells us that God speaks in unknown tongues just like our recreated spirits do, and then it goes on the tell us that praying in unknown tongues produces a **rest**, a **refreshment** or a **revival.** There have been times where praying in tongues has brought peace in the midst of a storm in my life, and there have been other times when speaking in tongues has caused me to shout victory and feel more ecstatic than a conqueror!

Acts 3:19

*Repent ye therefore, and be converted, that your sins may be blotted out, **when the times of refreshing shall come from the presence of the Lord;***

Chapter 6

Life as God has it

John 10:10

The thief comes not, but for to steal, and to kill, and to destroy: **I am come that they might have life,** *and that they might have it more abundantly.*

"Zoe" is the Greek term for life in this text, and it literally translates to **the divine life of God** or **the God kind of life** or **life as God has it.** Jesus not only wants us to have Zoe, but he also wants it to overflow from within us or spill over on to others. This is eternal life, and it abides in our born-again spirit. From deep within our recreated spirit, we can release Zoe into the lives of others or into earth's atmosphere through preaching and through prayers, praise and worship. When our words are in agreement with God's Word, Zoe comes forth from us and lives change when it's received. This overflowing of life in us can sometimes be perceived and felt by others who come in contact with us. Some may call it a light, a glow or an ore, but we know it as the life of God in us. Have you ever had someone tell you that there's something different about you but they can't put their finger on what it is? That's the life of God radiating from our spirit man occupying the earth.

John 6:63 NLT

The spirit alone gives eternal life. Human effort accomplishes nothing, and the very words I have spoken to you are spirit and life.

1 Corinthians 15:45

*And so it is written, The first man Adam was made **a living soul**; the last Adam was made **a life giving spirit**.*

We have to set our minds way beyond Eden. Adam experienced great glory because of his sinless state until he fell; we, however, have a greater glory. Furthermore, it's impossible for us to fall, thanks to God! Adam was made a living soul, implying that he operated through his senses and as long as he remained sinless, he lived in an elevated state. His mental capabilities were significantly more superior than those of mankind today; recall how he named every animal and insect and spoke of their attributes. He walked and talked with God through his natural senses while he remained sinless. But the last Adam—meaning Jesus Christ—was a life-giving spirit and we who are born again conform to his image and likeness. **We are life-giving spirits with the mind of Christ. We are one spirit with God. Out of our spirit flow the rivers of life.** If we renew our minds to all of this truth and speak it in faith, a great awakening would take place globally.

2 Corinthians 3:6

Who also hath made us able ministers of the new testament; not of the letter, but of the spirit: for the letter kills ***but the spirit gives life.***

Because of this new birth, God has given us the divine ability to speak life into bags of bones and dry lands. However, we must first be quipped with full knowledge of the new birth. Then, as our minds are renewed to this truth, we must boldly declare what God has done by conforming us to His very image and likeness. Yes, we sin in our flesh and commit mistakes that God is not pleased with. However, this is not with our born-again spirit. Therefore, we must be careful and walk in fear of the Lord because he abides in us and he cherishes our sinless spirit. We are unique because we simultaneously occupy two dimensions while being only separated by God's Holy Word.

*(For the word of God is quick, and powerful, and sharper than any two edged sword, **piercing even to the dividing asunder of soul and spirit**, and of the joints and marrow, and is a discerner of the thoughts and intents of the heart. Hebrews 4:12)*

The soul was our leader at birth, and it connects us with the aspects of our physical life on earth through our five senses. This is the part of us that we've used for learning and feeling and making decisions. This is the birth of the flesh that Jesus talked about in John 3:6. The birth of the spirit that Jesus talked about in that verse is that born-again part of us which is one with the Holy Spirit and abides in another dimension; only through the Word of God can there be fellowship between them. That is why it's so important to ensure agreement with these truths in our minds; then the heavenly place that our spirit resides in can also occupy our physical life. And as we fill ourselves with this revelation, it will start overflowing to the dry regions of our soul and mind and they will submit to the mind of Christ, which is the mind of our born-again spirit. When this happens, we will start changing things in this world by advancing God's kingdom on earth. As we speak the truth to our spirit man, he brings revelations to our minds. **As we confess these truths about our spirit man as our own, it gives our spirit**

preeminence. That is the natural man bowing down to the spiritual man. There exists a natural part of us and a supernatural part of us; both have to merge so that the supernatural life that is inside us will glorify God on earth as it does in heaven.

Romans 8:2

For the law of the Spirit of life in Christ Jesus hath made me free from the law of sin and death.

Romans 8:10

And if Christ be in you, the body is dead because of sin; but the Spirit is life because of righteousness.

2 Peter 1:4

Whereby are given unto us exceeding great and precious promises: that by these ye might be partakers of the divine nature, having escaped the corruption that is in the world through lust.

I cannot stress enough on how beneficial it is to meditate on these powerful truths about our born-again spirit man because according to 2 Peter 1:4, he will initiate **Godlike growth** in your life. Once we understand that we are **spirit**

first with **divine intellect** and with God's **divine seed** in us that lets his **divine life** to flow from us, then we will experience **Godlike growth in this life.** I agree with Peter that these promises are exceedingly great and precious—just think about all the trials that Jesus went through at Calvary to ensure that we gain this beautiful spiritual baptism. Think about what it means to be one with the precious Holy Spirit. Faith in these promises will lead us to be partakers in God's divine nature; being partakers implies that we will all share in it together as the body of Christ.

Chapter 7

Will the real you stand up

I remember in the initial years of walking closely with Jesus, I invested a significant amount of my time speaking in tongues and one day, while driving home from work, my spirit man shouted out "JESUS!" full of joy and excitement. I told the Lord that the man inside me is out of control, and the Holy Spirit softly said, **"don't say that because that's the real you!"** The Bible teaches us that **God is a Spirit** and that if we are made in his image and likeness, we are spirits first. This might seem daunting to us now because we cannot discern our real person yet. **This is why the Holy Spirit commissioned me to write this book to help us develop unity with ourselves.**

Gen 1:26

And God said, **Let us** *make man in our image, after our likeness:*

There is perfect unity within the Godhead. The usage "let us" implies **that the Father** and **the Son** and **the Holy**

Spirit speak here as one. Before we develop unity with ourselves, we must begin with the **"I principle"** and **"speak in plural"** about ourselves. This simply means that I am a spiritual being and my born-again spirit is the real me. So, I will take God's written truths about my spirit man and confess it with faith in my entire being, spirit, soul, and body. This will cause me to look at the things not seen for they are eternal. Let's start looking at ourselves as God looks at us and in accordance with our spirit man. The first part of this book is designed to lead us to **believe these truths in our hearts** and now we must **confess them with our mouths. Please understand that I am not saying that we are God. We will never be God. But we are of his divine seed and with his divine nature in our spirits.**

Confessions

Ephesians 4:24 I am holy

Ephesians 4:24 I am righteous

1John 3:9 I am sinless

1John 3:9 I am born of God's seed

1John 4:17 As he is in heaven, so am I in this world

1Corithians 2:16 I have the mind of Christ

2Peter 1:4 I partake of God's divine nature

Colossians 3:10 I am renewed with supreme intelligence daily

Acts 1:8 I am full of divine power

1Corithians 15:45 I am a life giving spirit

1Corithians 2:16 I discern all things

1Corithians 6:17 I am one with the Holy Spirit

2Corithians 5:17 Old things have passed away, all things have become new

Romans 6:4 I walk in newness of life

Romans 8:1 There is no condemnation in me

Ephesians 5:8 I am light in the Lord

John 3:8 I am like the wind traveling wherever I please

Ephesians 2:6 I am seated in heavenly places

Ephesians 1:3 I am blessed with all spiritual blessing in heavenly places

Ephesians 2:10 I am God's masterpiece created in Christ Jesus to do good works

These verses seem more comprehensible now. They are referring to our born-again spirit man, and as we come into agreement with the fact that our spirit is as much us as our mind and body, unity emerges that frees our spirit man to release divine life and grant revelation to our entire being! The key is to release our spiritual life into our physical life through our words. **Death and life are in the power of the tongue** and **out of the overflowing of the heart, the mouth speaks.** When we fill our minds with truth about our spirit and then confess it with our mouths, it brings unity to our soul and spirit. Remember that the Word cuts and takes its position between our soul and spirit so that fellowship can occur in line with the truth (God's Word). As we continue this process of confession, it initiates a merging and our minds submit to the mind of Christ, which is the mind of our spirit man. Just as our spirit is one with the Holy Spirit, through submission, our minds become one with the mind of Christ. **These scriptures prove to us who has preeminence** and it won't be long before **our minds will adjust to the fact that our born-again spirit should be dominant and in**

control! Then, we will be able to **walk and live in the Spirit** as Paul stated in Galatians 5:25. Child of God, please read and meditate on this book daily and I promise it will change your life. It may not happen right away because changing the way we've been thinking for many years is bound to take some time. However, your efforts will be worth the fruit. Realizing our spiritual identity is important for our overall wellbeing because it brings us to a place of divine alignment.

Galatians 5:15

This I say then, Walk in the Spirit, and ye shall not fulfil the lust of the flesh.

Galatians 5:18

But if ye be led of the Spirit, ye are not under the law

Galatians 5:25

If we live in the Spirit, let us also walk in the Spirit.

Romans 8:14

For as many as are led by the Spirit of God, they are the sons of God.

You might say, "Wait a minute, that's the Holy Spirit being mentioned in these verses" and I would say to you" 1 Corinthians 6:17 states 'But he that is joined unto the Lord is one spirit.' God loves His family, and we are all members of this great family. In saying that our born-again spirit is one with the Holy Spirit, the Holy Spirit acts as the mighty provider of all the attributes of our Great God. The Holy Spirit is our source of wisdom, power, authority, love, and so much more. However, these virtues are channeled to us through our born-again spirit, who is the real you! As we live in our born-again spirit, we live in the Holy Spirit because they are one spirit but separate entities.

Chapter 8

Spiritual Clothing

Ephesians 4:24

> **And that ye put on the new man,** which after
> God is created in righteousness and true holiness.

I would like to draw your attention to how Paul asks us to **put on** our born-again spirit. As we learned earlier in this book, our recreated spirit abides in another dimension and can't be discerned; he must be revealed through revelation. So what Paul is asking of us is to **put him on our mind daily** by **studying him, confessing oneness with him** and **learning from him by way of revelation.** To put on a spiritual virtue or a spiritual person in the physical world is to let them occupy your mind by thinking and learning about them and learning from them and talking about them—in essence, wearing them on our minds. Consider the saying "put them in our hearts." Most times, when someone is in your heart, you reach out to them to converse. The principle applies in Ephesians 6:11, **Put on the whole armour** *of God, that ye may be able to stand against the wiles of the devil.*

Paul is telling us to put these virtues in our hearts to study them and apply them in our life (faith, hope, salvation, peace, truth, God's Word). We are again being told by Paul to study our born-again spirit and to try to live out our spiritual life in this evil world. Let's be clothed with the spiritual knowledge of who we really are in Christ with courage and fervor! Go back and read the confession section again!

Matthew 11;29

Take my yoke upon you, *and learn of me; for I am meek and lowly in heart: and ye shall find rest unto your souls.*

Here's this spiritual principle again, with Jesus telling us to put on his yoke. Along with putting on the yoke comes **"learn of me"** and doing as one sees him do. This is the same thing that Paul told us to do regarding our born-again spirit man—learn of him and set your heart to follow him as he follows the Holy Spirit.

Colossians 3:10

And have put on the new man, which is renewed in knowledge after the image of him that created him.

Here, we have it again. This must be instrumental to our spiritual welfare; it's similar to one day finding out who you really are and when you do, you realize that you are so much more than you could have ever imagined. This spiritual rebirth is available to all who will come to Jesus Christ for the remission of your sins and you shall receive the Holy Ghost.

If you are not born again and you want to experience this glorious life, say this prayer with me and mean it with everything that's in you.

> Lord Jesus I believe that you died on the cross for my sins and rose from the dead on the third day,
>
> Please forgive me and cleanse me from all sin and unrighteousness and every wicked thing I've done,
>
> I forgive all who have wronged me as I want God to forgive me and grant me eternal life,

I receive Jesus Christ as my Lord and Savior and I will follow him for the rest of my days

In Jesus' name I pray,

Amen.

If you make that prayer from the bottom of your heart, God will hear and answer you!

Welcome to the family of God!

9 781647 645472